T0053457

CONTEMPORARY PRAYERS

to whatever works

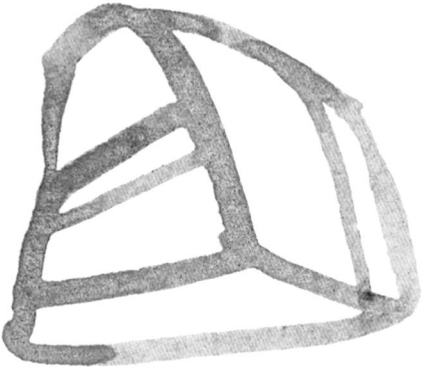

An Artist's Collection of
Prayers to Nothing-in-Particular

CONTEMPORARY PRAYERS *to whatever works*

HANNAH BURR

TILLER PRESS
New York London Toronto Sydney New Delhi

TILLER PRESS

An Imprint of Simon & Schuster, Inc.
1230 Avenue of the Americas
New York, NY 10020

Copyright © 2021 by Hannah Burr

All rights reserved, including the right to reproduce this book or portions thereof in any form whatsoever. For information, address Simon & Schuster Subsidiary Rights Department, 1230 Avenue of the Americas, New York, NY 10020.

First Tiller Press trade paperback edition March 2021

TILLER PRESS and colophon are trademarks of Simon & Schuster, Inc.

For information about special discounts for bulk purchases,
please contact Simon & Schuster Special Sales at 1-866-506-1949
or business@simonandschuster.com.

The Simon & Schuster Speakers Bureau can bring authors to your live event.
For more information or to book an event, contact the Simon & Schuster Speakers Bureau at 1-866-248-3049 or visit our website at www.simonspeakers.com.

Interior design by Jennifer Chung

Manufactured in China

10 9 8 7 6 5 4 3 2 1

Library of Congress Cataloging-in-Publication Data
Names: Burr, Hannah, 1973- author.
Title: Contemporary prayers to whatever works : an artist's collection of prayers to nothing-in-particular / Hannah Burr. | Description: New York : Tiller Press, 2021. | Includes bibliographical references. | Identifiers: LCCN 2020021257 (print) | LCCN 2020021258 (ebook) | ISBN 9781982154677 (paperback) | ISBN 9781982154684 (ebook) | Subjects: LCSH: Prayers.
Classification: LCC BL560 .B824 2021 (print) | LCC BL560 (ebook) | DDC 204/.33—dc23

LC record available at https://lccn.loc.gov/2020021257
LC ebook record available at https://lccn.loc.gov/2020021258

ISBN 978-1-9821-5467-7
ISBN 978-1-9821-5468-4 (ebook)

To

CONTENTS

Introduction *ix*
On Slow 1
Fast Brain 17
Nope 29
Stay Here 45
Dread 63
Others 79
Offering 95
Inner Kid 111
Way Through 131
New View 151
Yes 169
Acknowledgments *189*
Notes *191*
Index *193*

INTRODUCTION

This book is an artist's take on prayers, written in plain language to whomever or whatever works for you. It's one in a series intended for anybody, regardless of belief. It sidesteps the whole debate about what one personally feels connected to, and instead focuses on the act of connection itself.

The images in this book aren't supposed to resemble anything in particular. They have been paired at random with the phrases, and painted with acrylic gouache pigment on paper. They are abstract forms that can stand in for whatever you might want to address in a prayer or petition. What you address is your business: it could be a mythic warrior princess or a plastic bottle, Jesus or Great Spirit, or a force like gravity, art, or the ocean. Some prayers include other dash- or dot-like images, which you can fill in with whatever person, place, thing, or scenario is currently in heavy rotation in your thoughts and feelings.

Sections like "Yes" offer prompts for noting the action of prayer, expressions of gratitude, and a little creative brain-

storming. These are a means of redirecting thought when it tends to slide into shadow territory, particularly when the shadows begin to engulf and overwhelm. Play around with them and see how and when they work for you.

You don't have to understand or have a clear idea of what you believe in to pray; it can be fuzzy, and your experience may change over time. I find that the more I engage in prayer of this kind, the less I understand what I'm praying to and yet the more intimate the relationship becomes.

You also don't need anybody's permission or intercession to connect directly with ⊘. No one is more qualified than you, though others may be more familiar with the practice.

Lastly, this is a come-as-you-are affair. There's no need to be eloquent or pious to engage in prayer. I find it's best not to BS, sugarcoat, or be overly formal in my prayers. Honesty is the very medium of this whole process. Phrases like the ones in this book help me to touch ground and admit my smallness, and by so doing connect to a broader freedom and peace, similar to what I experience beside an expanse of ocean or looking up at a big sky.

I'm writing this introduction in April 2020, when the world is collectively experiencing alarming and sudden upheaval, over which we seem to have little to no control. We are a species in free fall with an uncertain future. This may have always

been true, but it is nearly impossible to ignore at this moment in history. These phrases were mostly written in response to personal circumstances at an earlier time, and yet strike me as highly relevant and practical for right now, too. May they assist you and those you love in navigating whatever is in front of you at present and surround you with in the details of your day.

ON SLOW

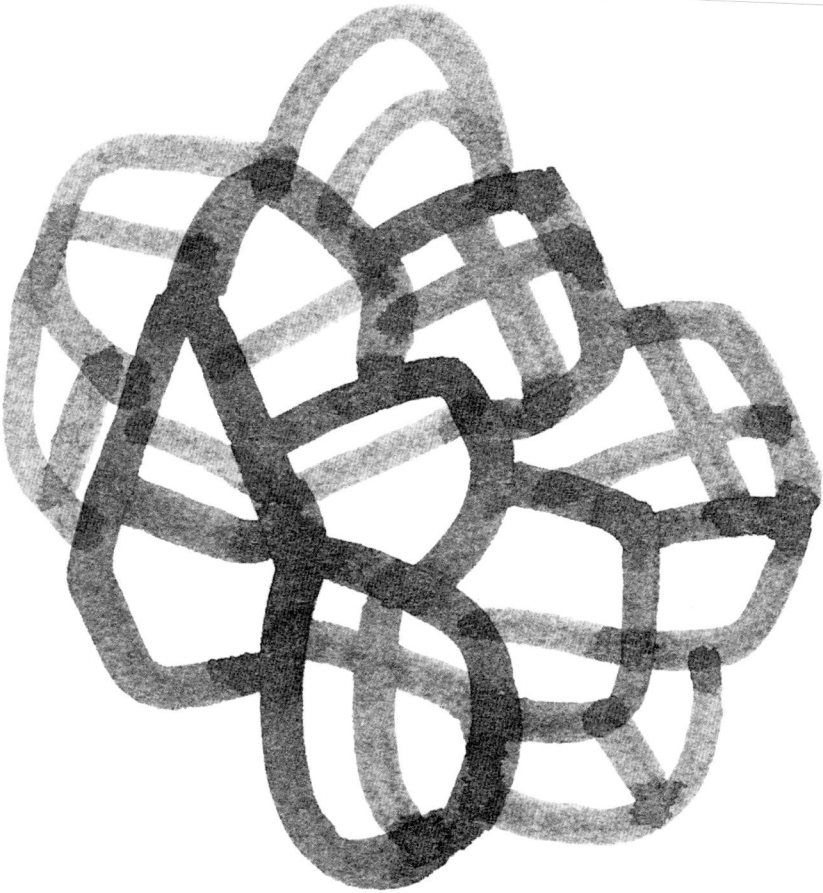

Quiet my mind, 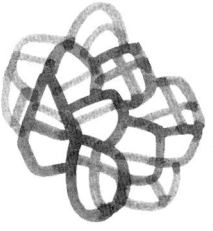 ,

and show me what's next.

Help me, ,

to think like a piece of wood,
or a plant.

Just for a little while.

Can you help me,

,

get off the couch?
Or, if I'm supposed to be resting here,
help me to let myself be,
and give myself a pass for now.

I'm tired and depleted.

, help me to rest.

Help me,  ,

to take in the specific arrangement of objects in front of me,

to really see the details.

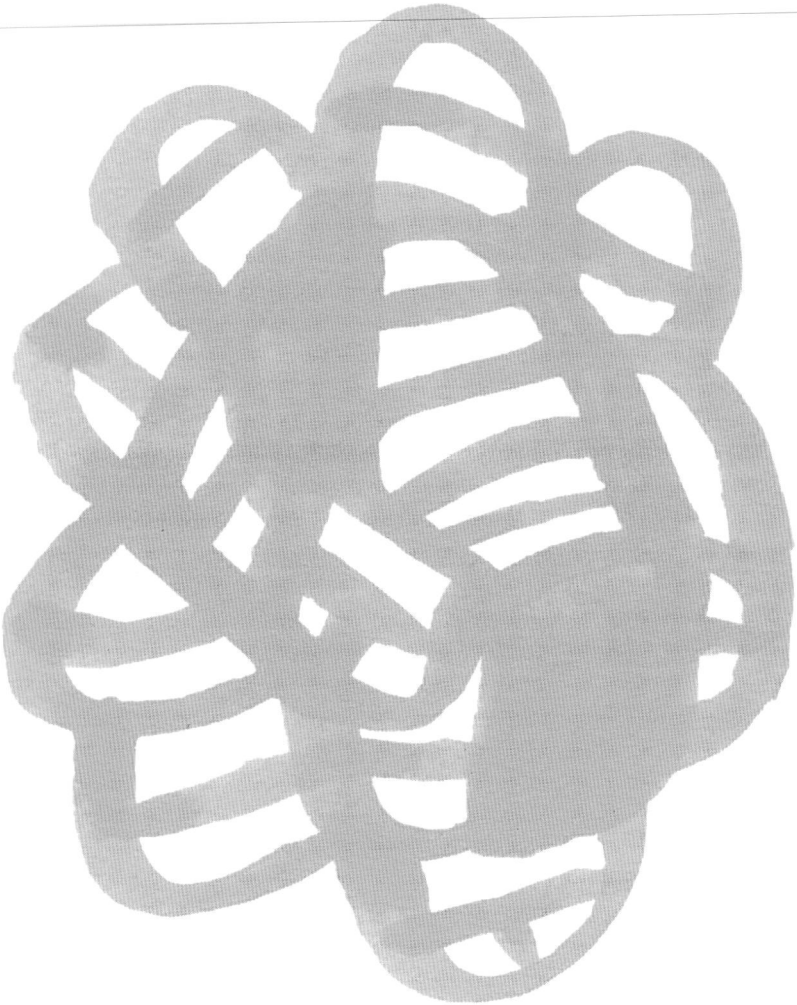

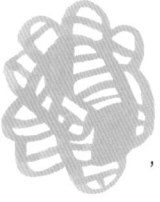

, show me how to listen to,

care for, and rest
in this only body I have.

, even in this completely
unrecognizable situation,

I'm feeling okay and trusting in you.

If you'd prefer I be wigging out,
please let me know.

FAST BRAIN

There's a code-red emergency going on
in this human brain of mine!

Please, 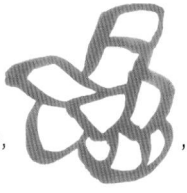 ,

help me to drop down into the
grounding shelter of the body.

I'm overwhelmed,  .

, I can't seem to

stay away from .

Please help!

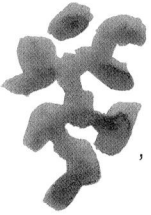

, please talk me down
off the ledge.

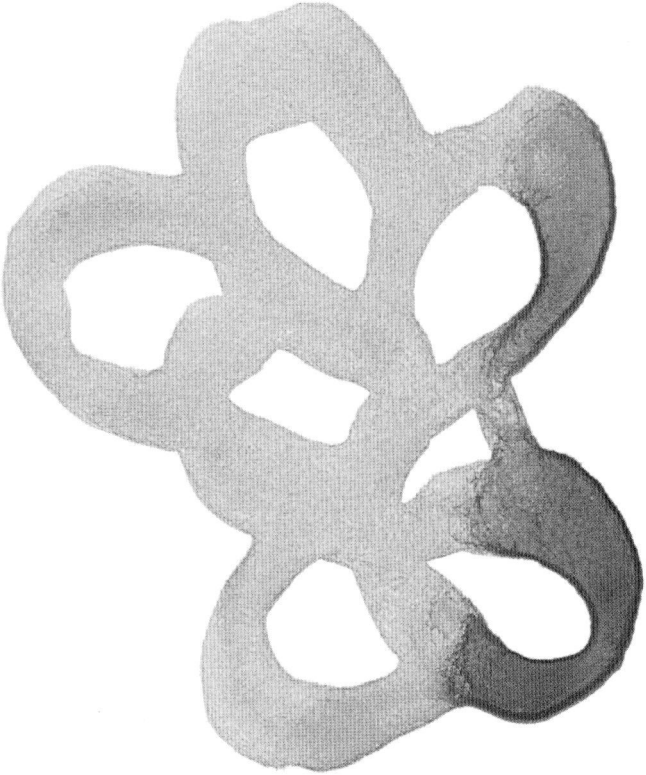

 , I need your help.

I'm in obsession and the brain won't stop!

Please direct my attention to
where you want it.

NOPE

What. The. F.

Not. Okay.

This is my prayer, 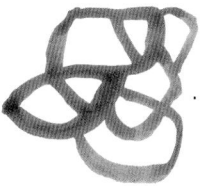 .

Everything feels ashen and gray.

Can you help me,  ,

to reconnect with joy
and delight?

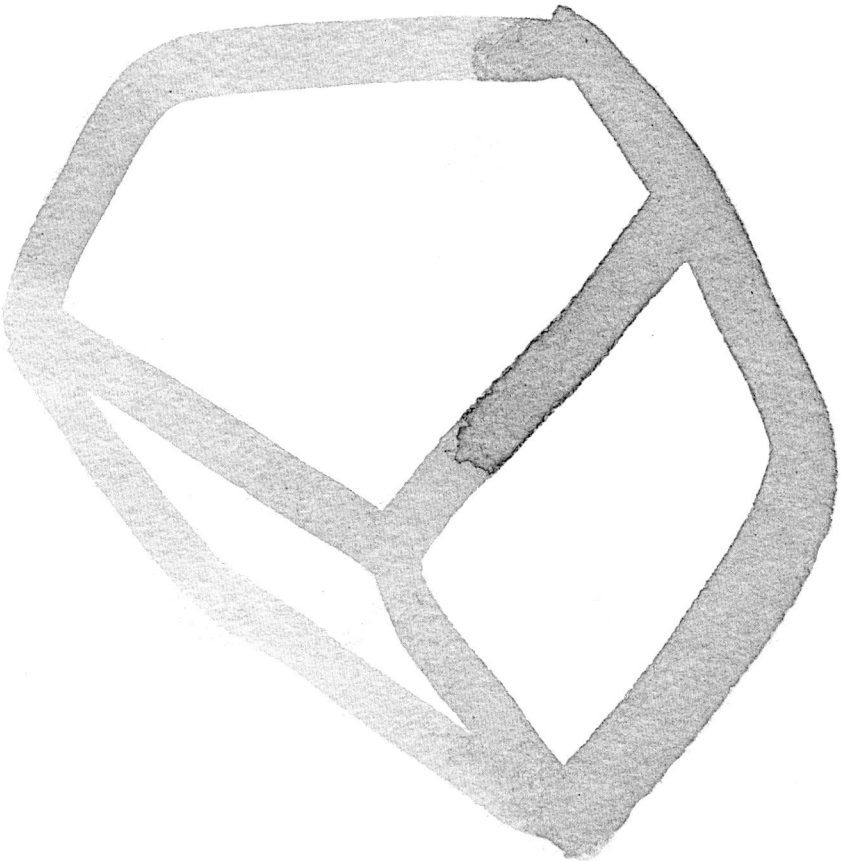

I gotta be honest, 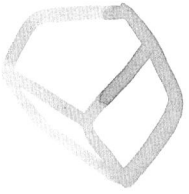 ,

this is a serious shit-storm
and I am not happy.

This is my honest and
only offering right now.

What an uncomfortable situation!

I can't seem to either swallow this
or spit it out.

See me through this,

please,  .

, I am in RESISTANCE.

Like a donkey pulling backward in full bray,
I am NOT going along smilingly here.

It's a real throw-down.

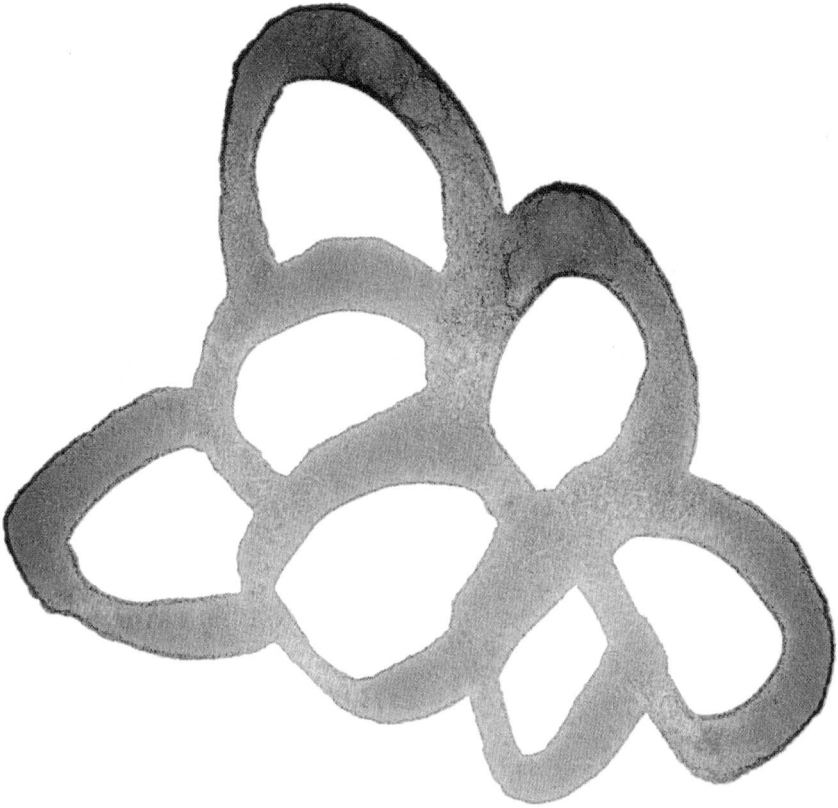

That was not okay,  .

I keep replaying it.

Help me to let this move through me
without making things worse.

My hackles are seriously UP.

Please, 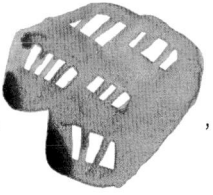 ,

surround and protect me
from my own disturbed thinking.

STAY HERE

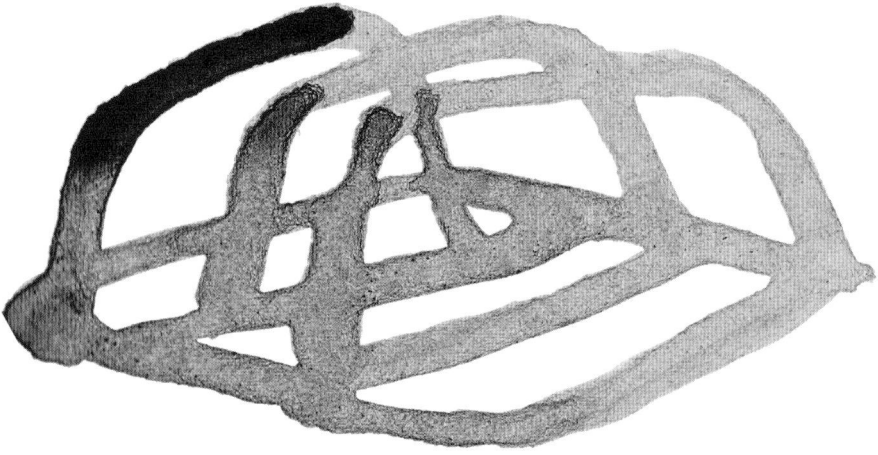

Help me,  ,

to be present for  ,

fully here and in my body.

Help me notice the details,  ,

the ones that matter,
the subtle sparkly underlayer to things.

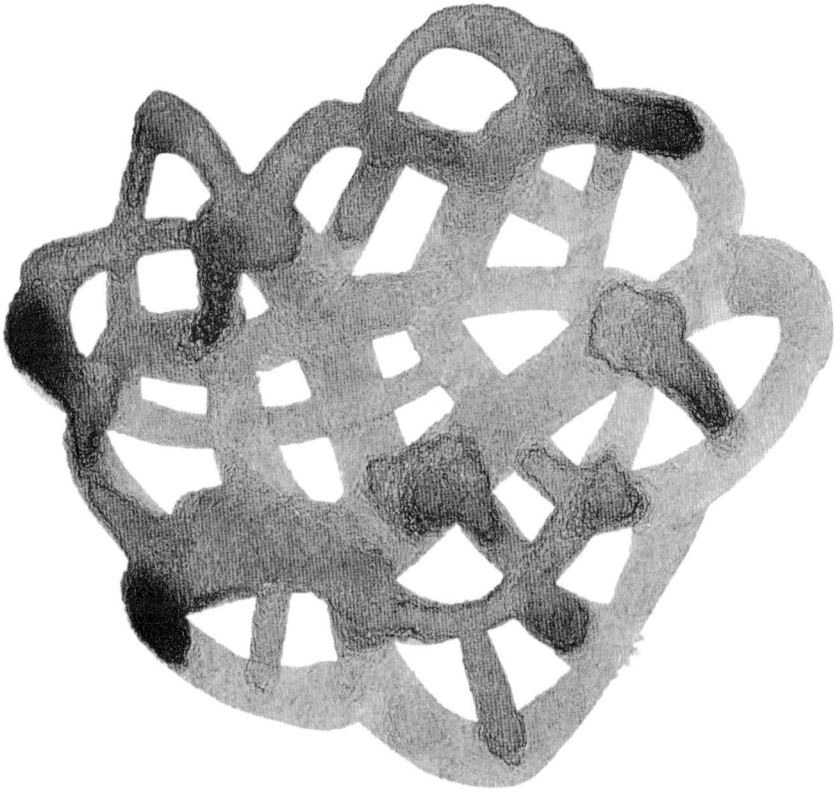

Thank you, 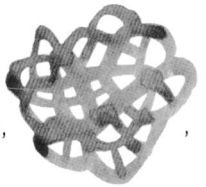 ,

for being the tree in my yard
and the chair that I'm sitting in.*

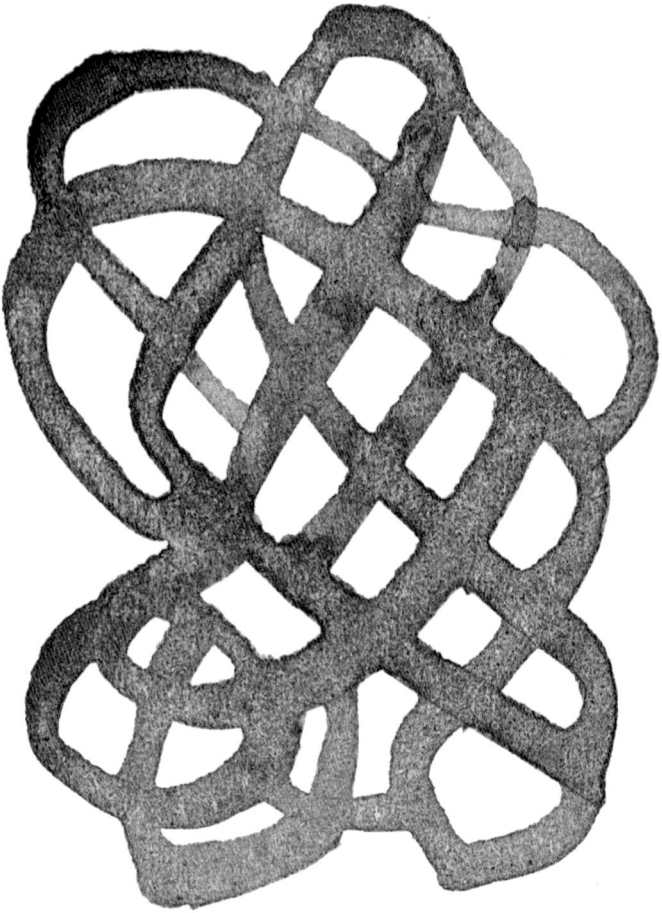

Help me,  ,

to find you via the senses,
right here and now.

Here's what I see: 

Here's what I smell: 

Here's what I hear: 

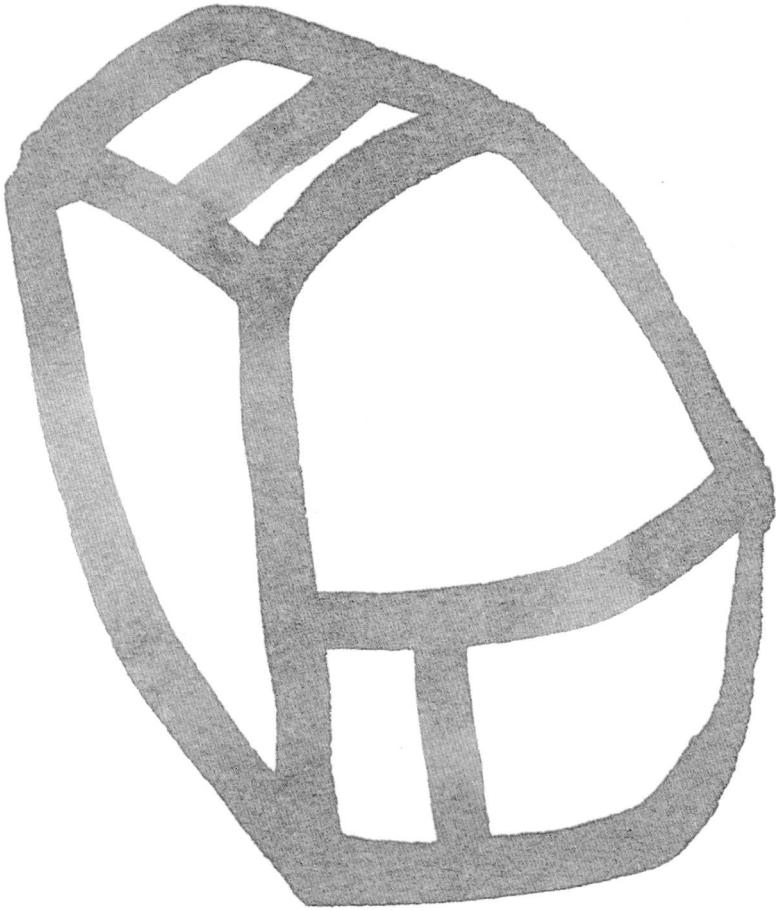

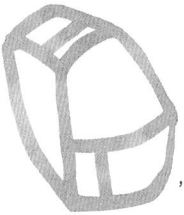

, help me drop the idea
of past and future

for the what and who that is here,
right in front of me, just now.

Thank you,  ,

for being the very situation.

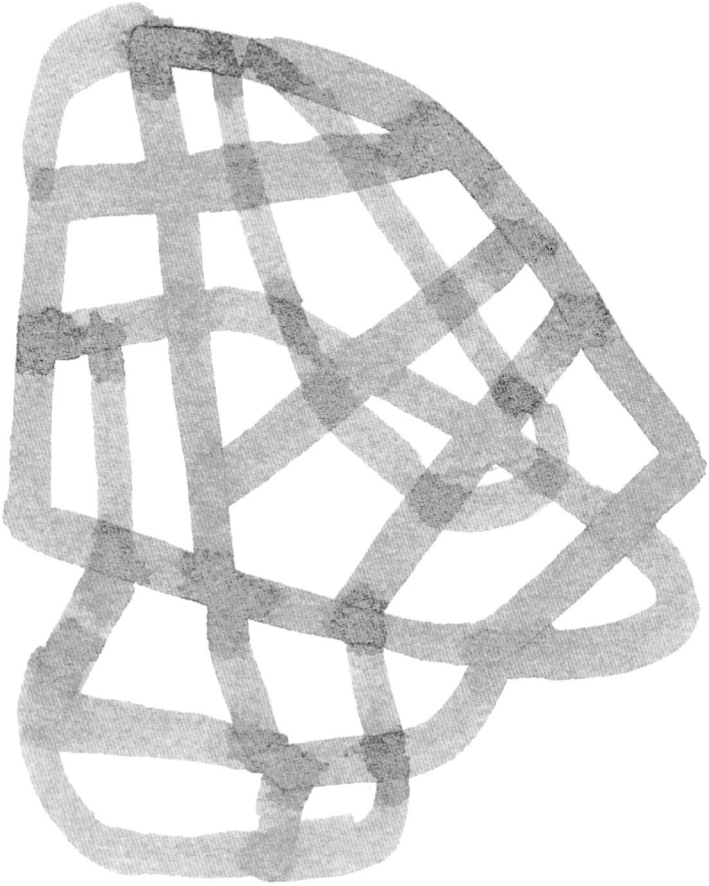

, here is where I felt your
presence and love

in the day: 

Help me,  ,

to reconnect with
what matters and what lasts.

Help me not to try to figure out
what these are.

DREAD

Okay, 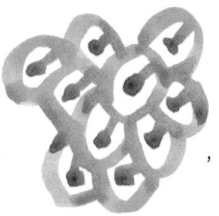 ,

I'm officially spooked!

Help bring me back down
into the body and legs.

Thank you.

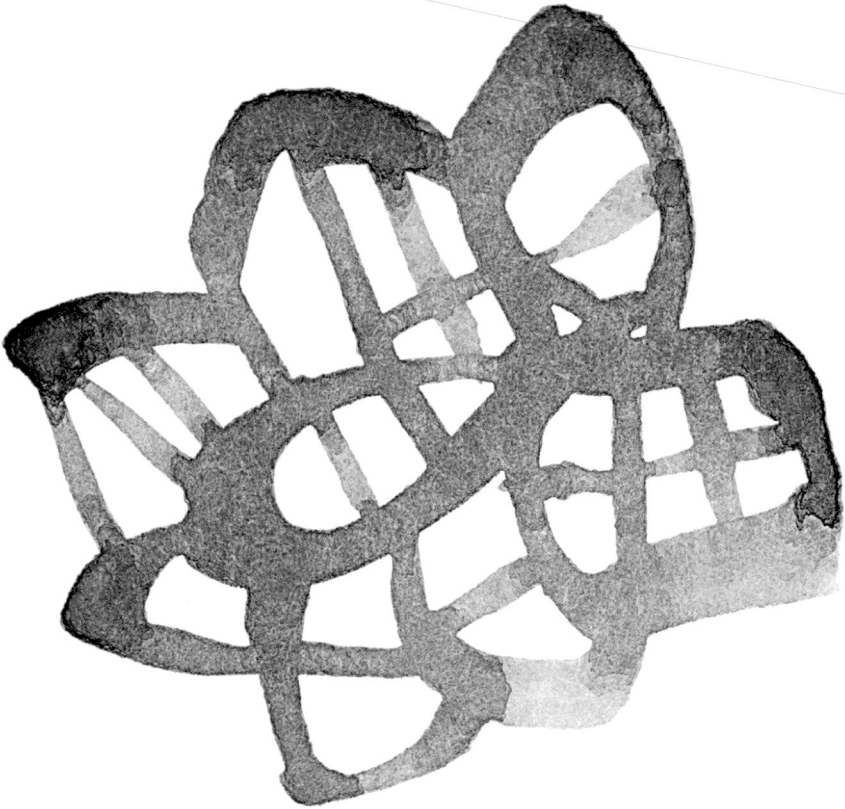

My whole system feels wrecked:
shaky, jittery, and off-balance.

Please,  ,

smooth out this whole vibe going on.

Thanks.

Remind me,  ,

that this, like everything,
won't last forever.

That I've been in a similar place before
and it worked out okay.

In my thinking and stories, 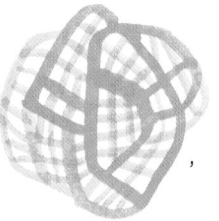 ,

this is a disaster.

Can you help me see otherwise?

Show me,  ,

the difference between humiliation

and humility.

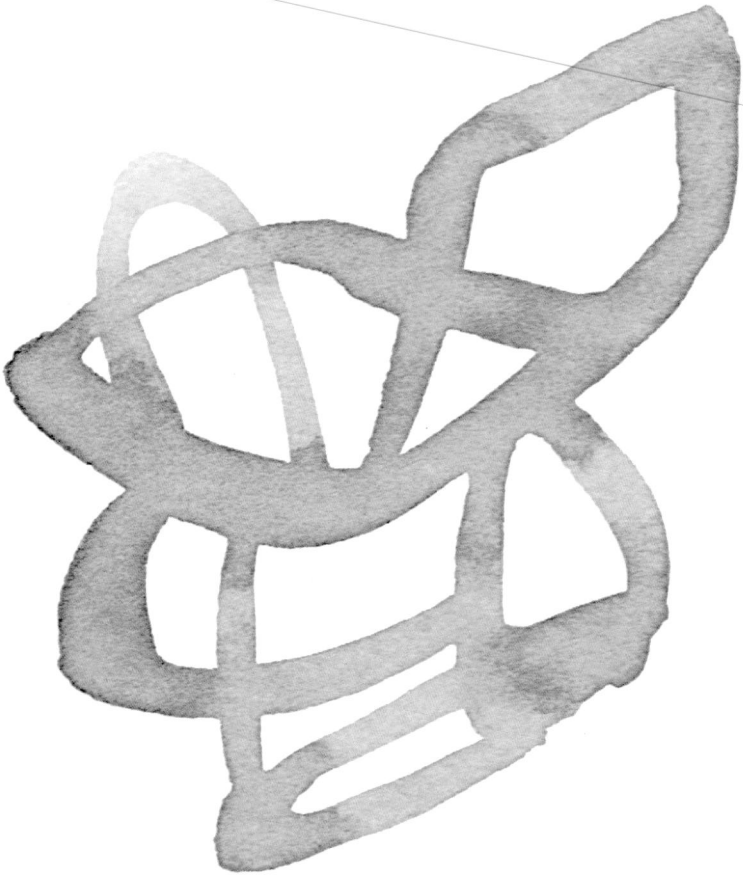

I've lost my sense of humor,  .

I'd love to find myself laughing
at something at silent-laugh
or snort-level today.

Thank you.

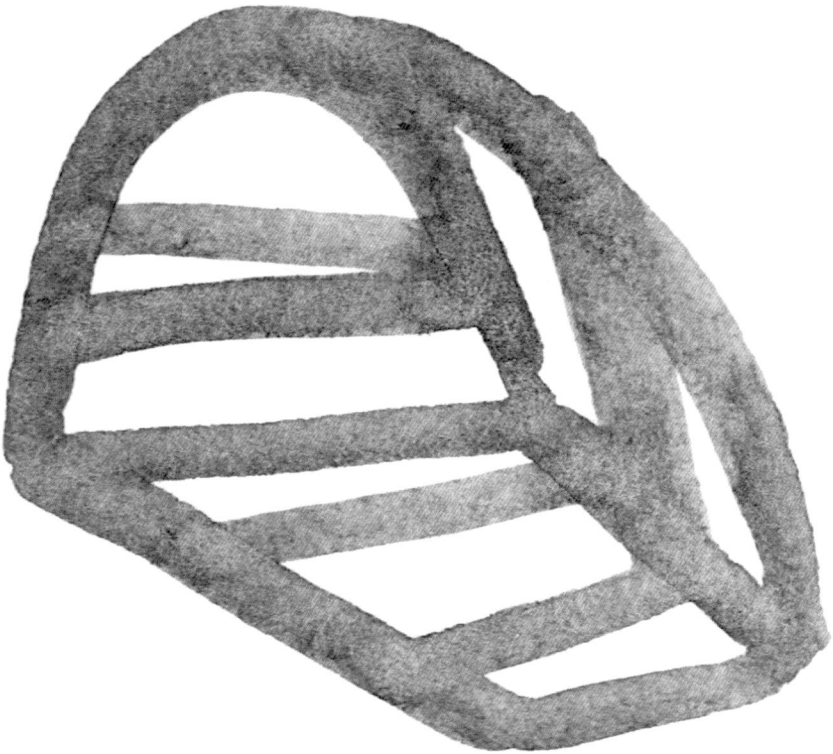

I leave with you,  ,

the following
disquieting concerns:  .

And I thank you for 

and  .

OTHERS

Help me,  , to let others be.

Help me,  , to let myself be.

Please guide and
inspire this  ,

and everyone involved.

Help it flow.

Make it astonishingly easy,
and also delightful for all of us.

I keep wanting to
change, fix,
or influence .

Please, ,

help me stay in my
own Hula-Hoop here.

Show me how to be
supportive here, 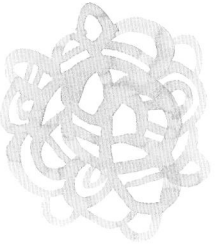 ,

and how to "shut it"
when I might otherwise cause harm.

Help me to enjoy my life,  ,

the people I meet,
the things I do.

, help me to drop the
hero complex

and show me how to
serve without fanfare.

Help me, 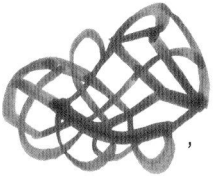 ,

to be free of attachment or aversion,

while still continuing to care.*

OFFERING

Help me,  ,

to let all of this be,

even the squelchy parts.

I know  isn't working

but I'm not yet willing to let it go.

Help me, 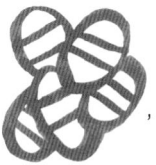 , to be willing.

, I really don't want to,

but I offer up  to you.

I leave  in your care

and trust this will work out okay,
even if I can't imagine how right now.

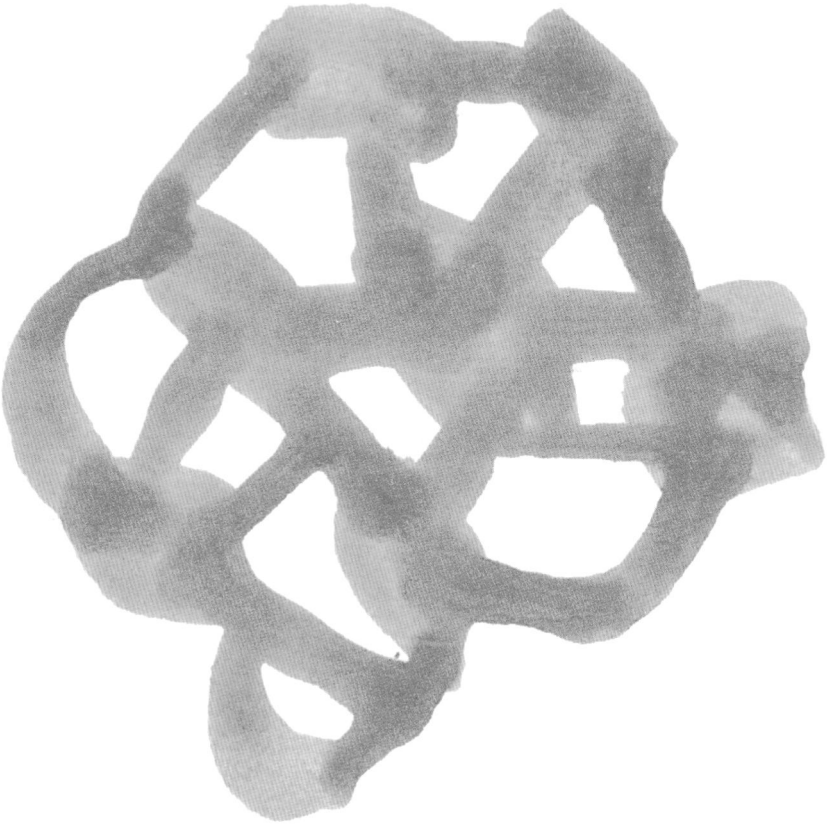

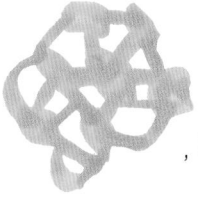

, help me to pry open this death grip

I have on  .

Please redirect my focus.

 , help me stand in the truth

and let go of the outcome.

Here,  ,

is what I place on the makeshift

altar/drop-off-the-cliff edge: 

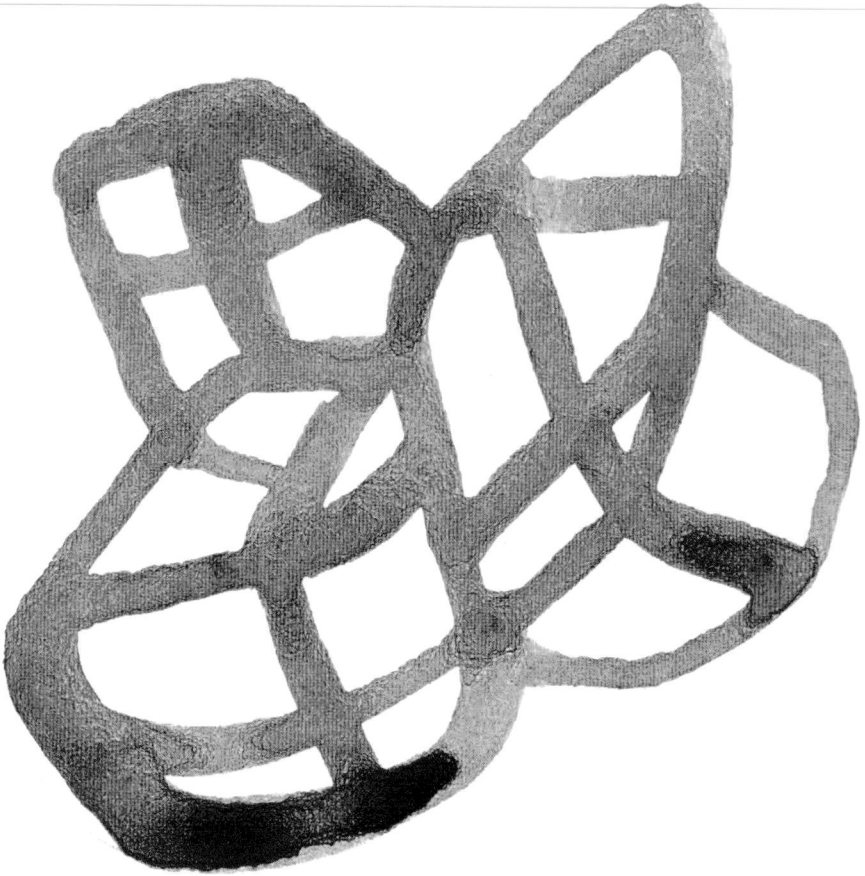

Please, 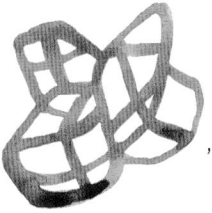 ,

be the doer of this day.*

INNER KID

How,  , may I treat myself

like I might treat a baby otter,
a baby cheetah,
or a wobbly spring lamb?

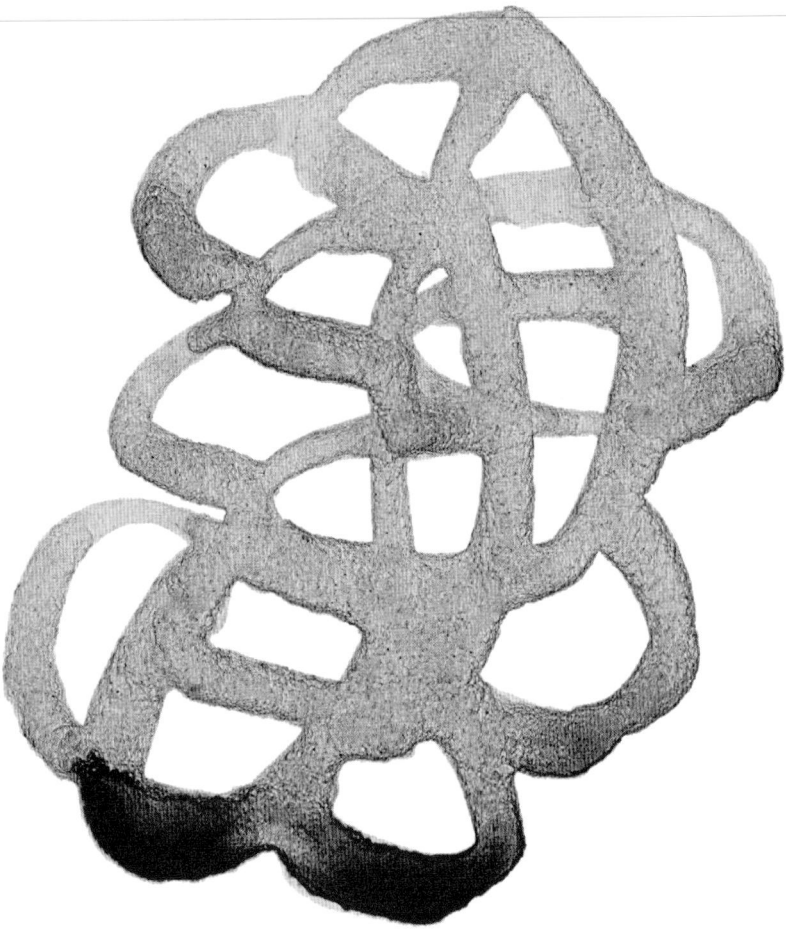

Help me, 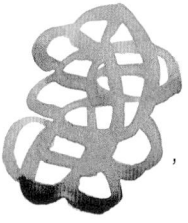 ,

to see everyone around me,
and myself,

like toddlers bumbling around
playing dress-up.

I'd love to feel wonder
and awe,  ,

like a kid—
please make it so!

Help me,  ,

to slip out of this jaded,
cynical, and blamey attitude

and into something that feels more
right-sized and comfortable.

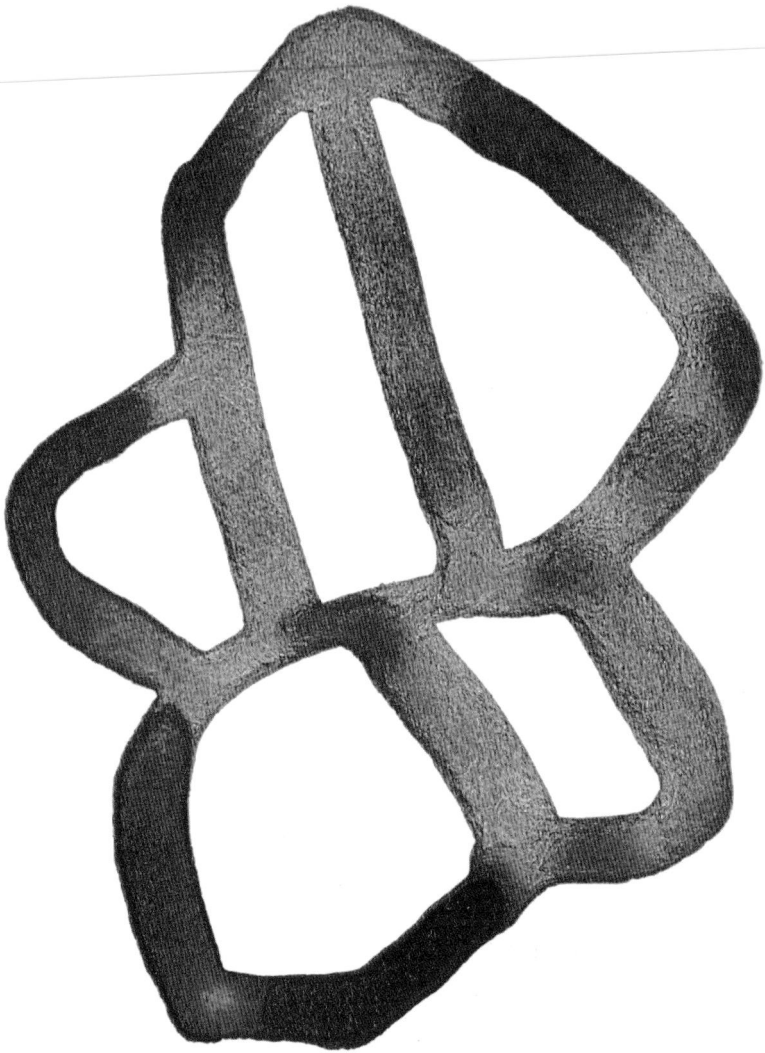

Show me, 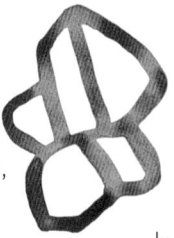 ,

how to say YES

even to the messy,

the ugly, and the awkward

in myself and in others.

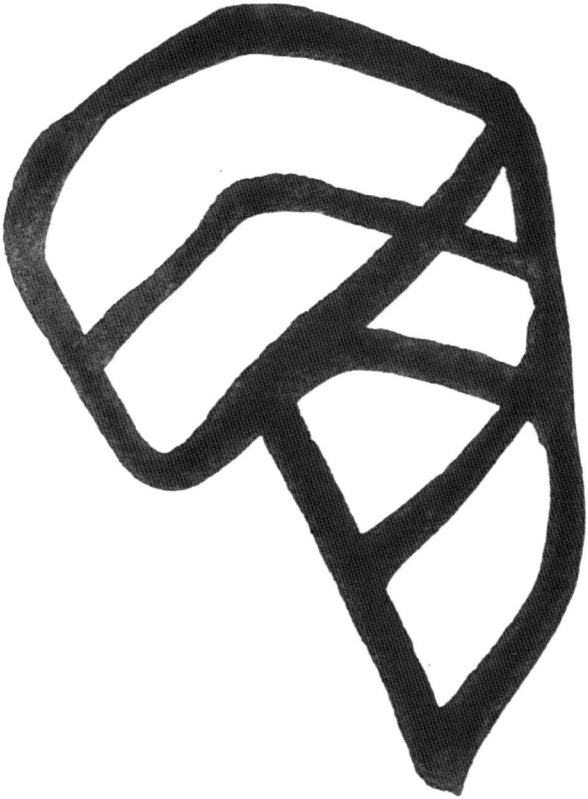

, I'm feeling small
and separate.

Please plug me back in.

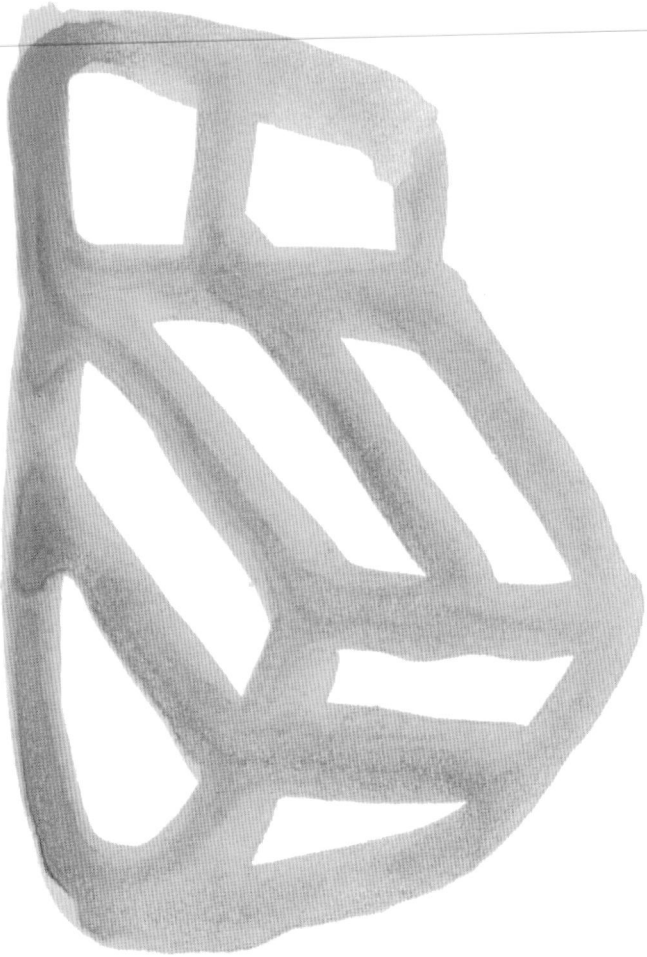

May I trust you, 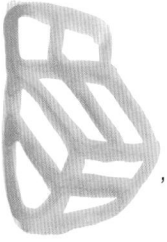 ,

and take you with me all places.*

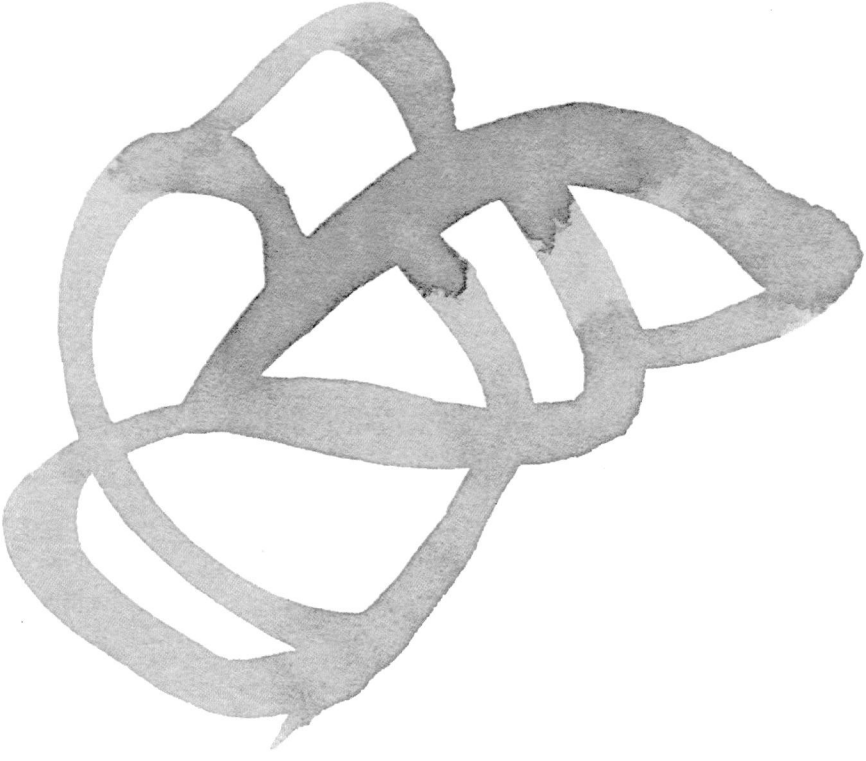

, you are in charge and,

weirdly somehow,
beyond my understanding.

Please show me how to be in flow
and connected to you
throughout this day.

, will you help me

fall in love with my own life,
my own body,

my own self?

WAY THROUGH

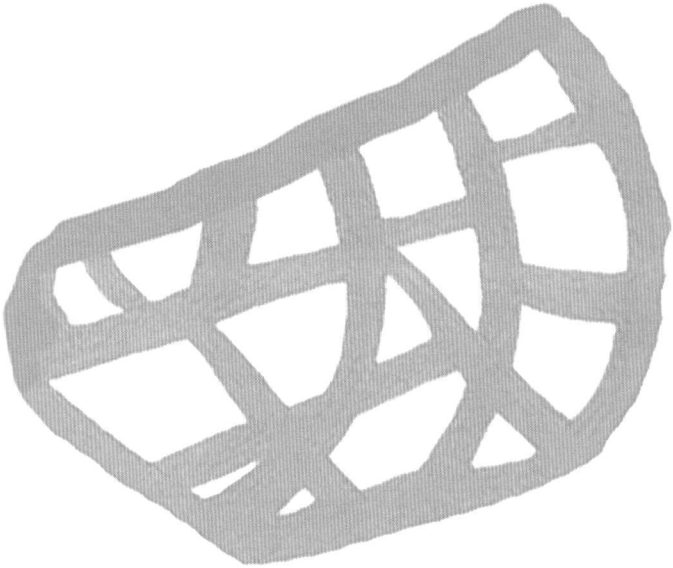

I'm at a crossroads 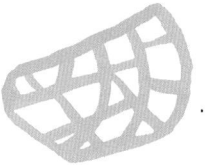 .

Which way should I go?

There's got to be a better way,  .

Will you show me?

, I've never been here before.

Are you still here with me?

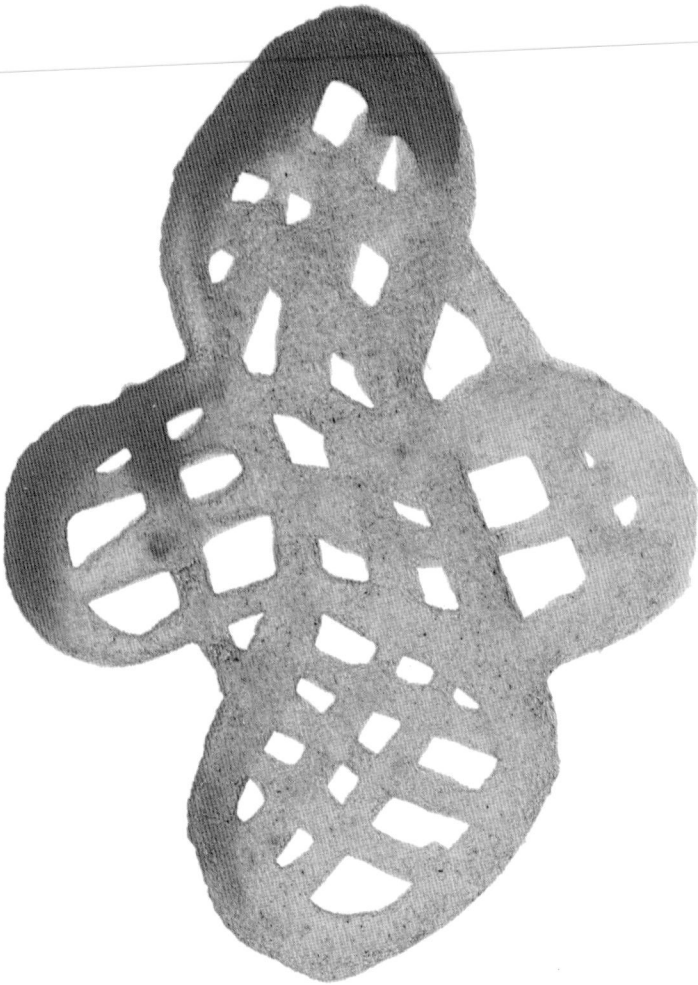

, help me to find my way

through the unfamiliar light
of this situation/day.

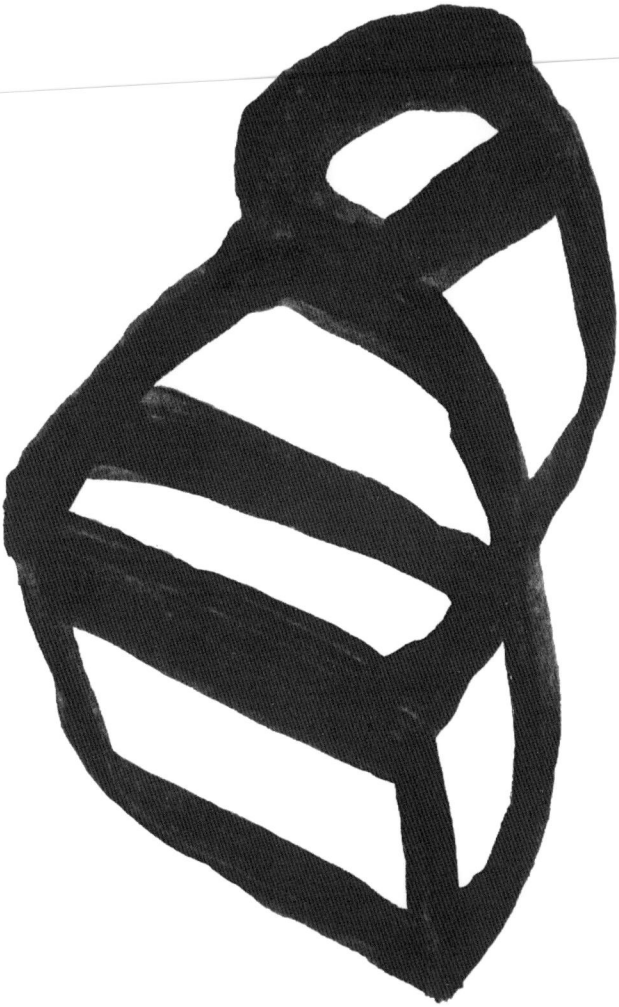

Up is down
and down is up!

Where are you,  , in all of this?

I'd like to feel your presence
palpably with me,
in and all around me.

, it feels like things have changed
and they might not ever
be the same.

I want you as my through line.

Please be with me from now on.

Despite all the tantalizing distractions,

I will look for you,  ,

in this day.

Please,  ,

go before me into this interaction
so that you're there before I get there;

may I trust in your presence
in every detail of the
unfolding situation.

Wow.

This is heavy.

Help me stay with this.

Help me move through.

NEW VIEW

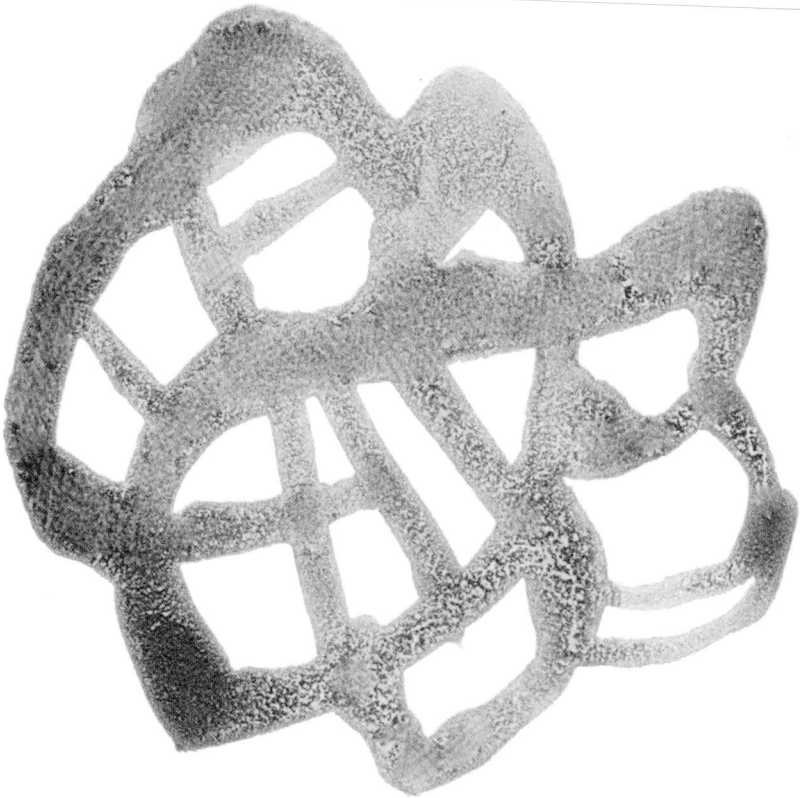

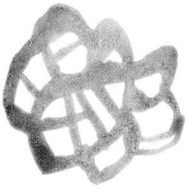

, how might this be
the best thing

that could be happening to me?

Help me to see this with fresh eyes.

Illuminate my view, 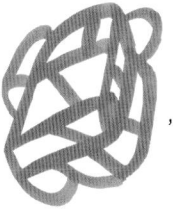 ,

surprise and inspire me—please!

Help me,  ,

to sit back and
let all of these events unfold

with their strange and uncanny precision,
as they do,

no meddling needed from me.

 , I'm taking this super personally.

Can you bring a new perspective wherein
I'm not the center of all orbits?

Help me, 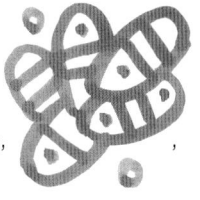 ,

to see beauty in details today,
even in trash blowing by.

Let me see its singularity and perfection.

Help me to be truly honest
with myself, 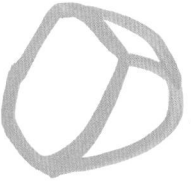 .

Help me to look at things without
distortion, blinders, or special filters.

Where things seem solid
and fixed in place, 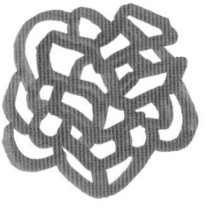 ,

help me to see the possibility of
motion and change.

Where I see a small part up close,
help me to also see a vast expanding.

Inspire me,  ,

toward what you want for me.

Help me to lose interest in what doesn't
ultimately serve your purposes.

YES

Help me, 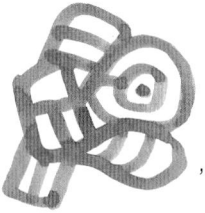 ,

to want what I have.

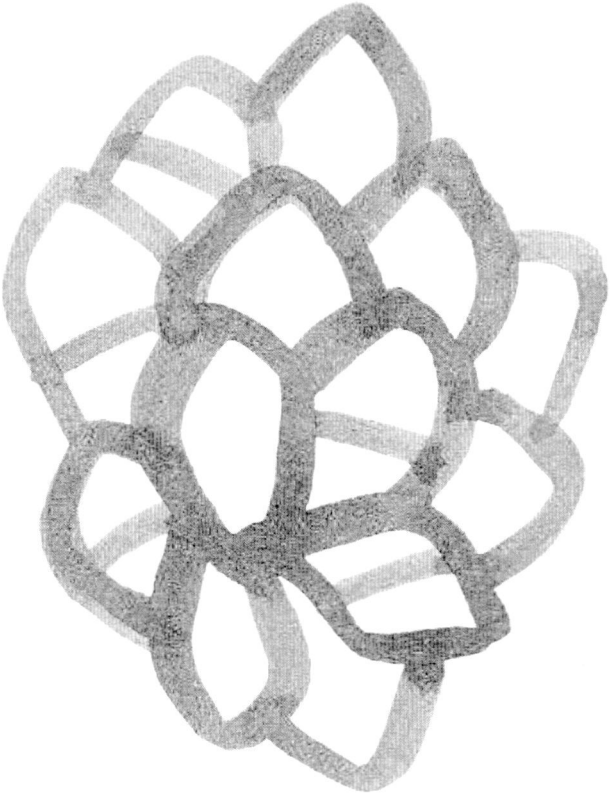

Help me, 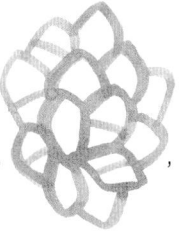 ,

to enjoy the ride:

the twists and turns,
bumps and all.

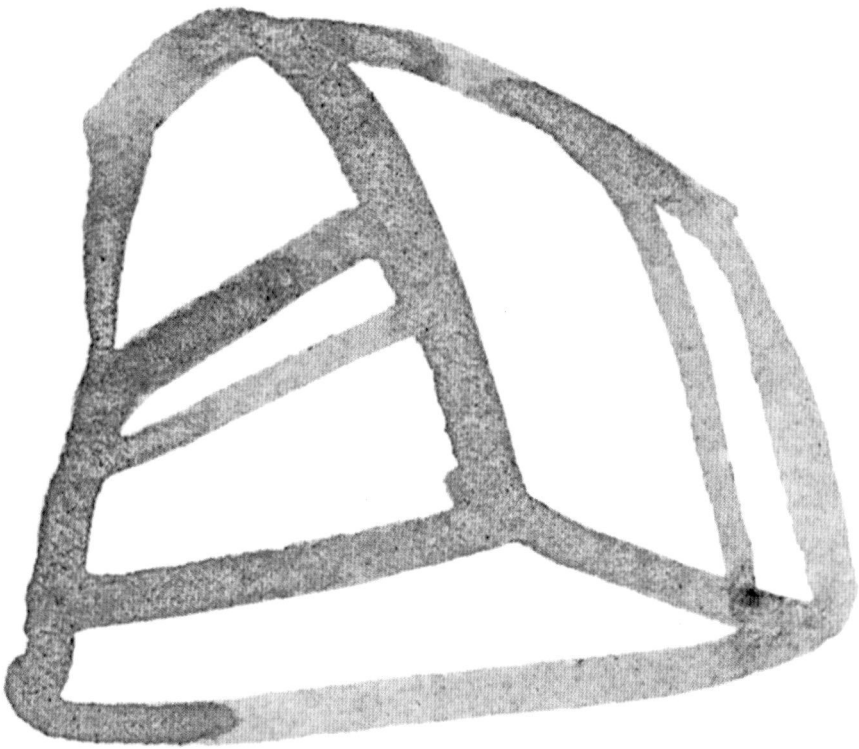

Thank you,  ,

for the dreamlike adventure of this life.

Help me to be curious, to get into it
instead of shying away from it.

, here's what I loved

about today:

These,  ,

are my absolute favorite things

in the world: 

Thank you!

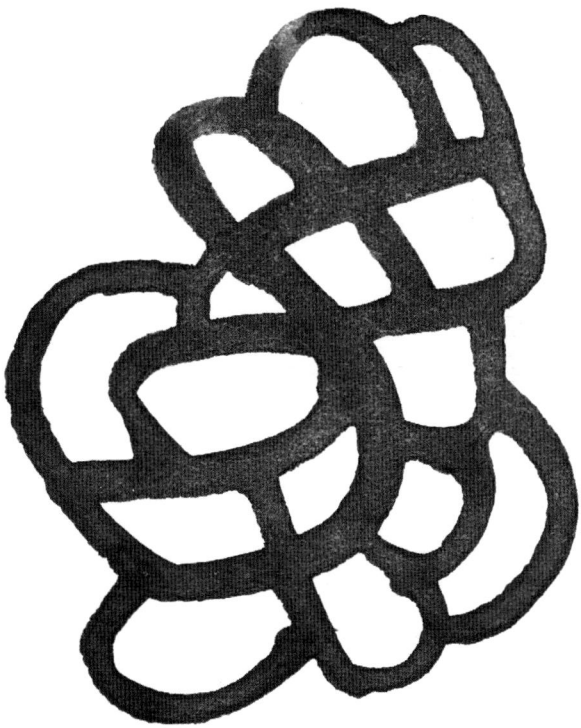

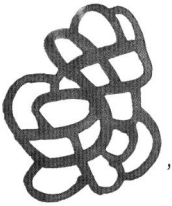

, I remember the following

joy-filled moments:

More like this, please!

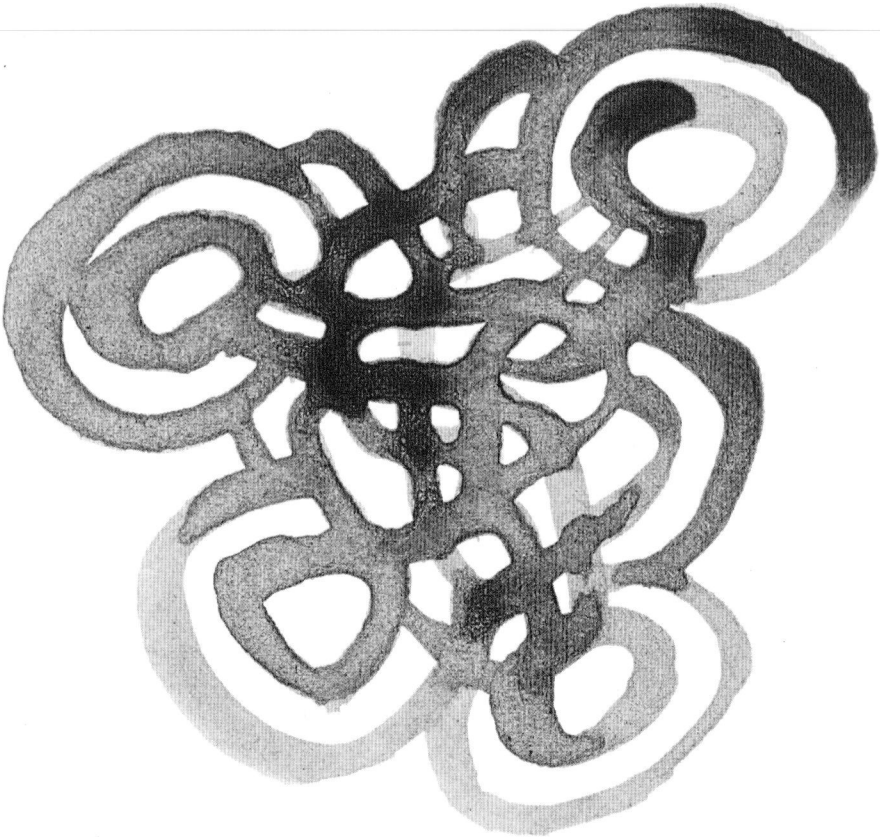

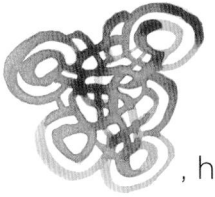

, here's what I want to

acknowledge and

appreciate about today:

, and ,

and ,

and also .

Thank you,  ,

for this particular weather pattern

and its interesting qualities of  ,

 , and  .

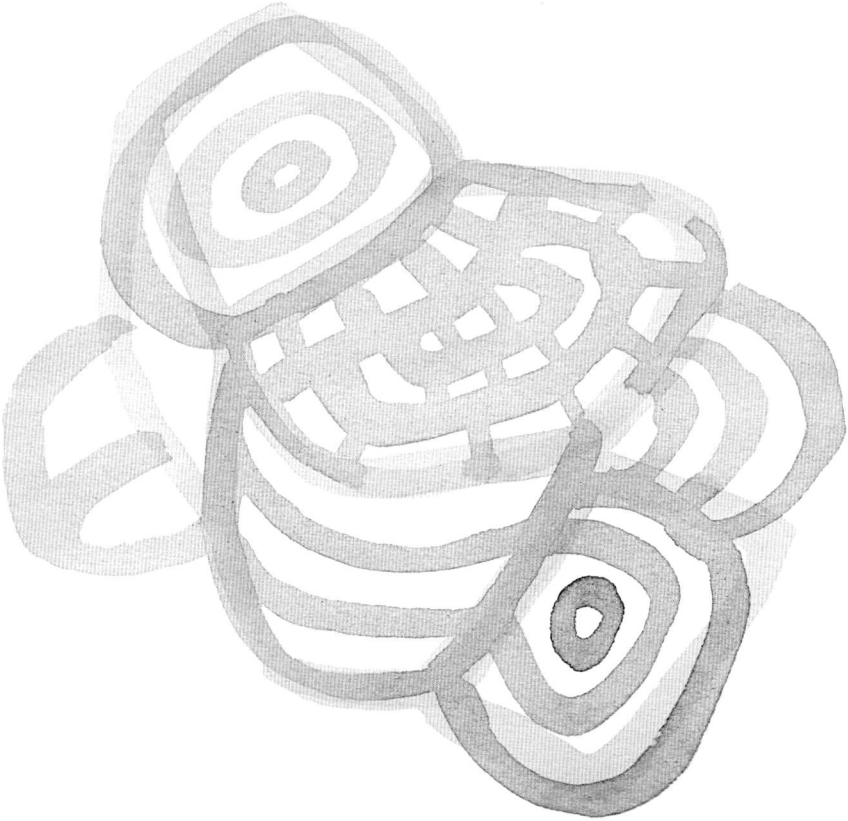

I'm grateful right now, ,

for .

Today,
I would love to experience ,

, and .

ACKNOWLEDGMENTS

Thank you Thank you Thank you

NOTES

51 This prayer was originally printed in *Contemporary Prayers to * [whatever works]* by Hannah Burr in 2013.

93 Adapted from the *Visuddhimagga Buddhaghosa*, a treatise on Buddhism written in the fifth century CE by Buddhaghosa and referenced often in contemporary Buddhist writing.

109 This prayer was originally printed in *Help me [ ], do the thing* by Hannah Burr in 2016.

125 This phrasing is inspired by the poem "love is a place" by e. e. cummings.

INDEX

A

acceptance, 57, 89, 97, 149
acknowledge, 183
addiction, 23
adventure, 175
all around, 141
altar, 77, 107
anxiety, 65
appreciate, 183
ashen, 33
attachment, 93, 103
attention, 27, 103
aversion, 93
awe, 117
awkward, 121

B

baby animals, 113
balance, 67
beauty, 161
being, 51, 57
better way, 133
beyond understanding, 127
blamey, 119
blinders, 163
body, 13, 19, 47, 65, 129
bray, 39
brink, 25
bumbling, 115
bumps, 173

C

care, 93, 101
chair, 51
change, 85, 143, 165
cheetah, 113
choice, 133
clarity, 11
cliff, 107
code-red, 19
collaboration, 83, 181, 187
comfortable, 119
compulsion, 23
concern, 77
connection, 61, 123, 127, 137, 141
constant, 143
control, 85, 103, 127
couch, 7
courage, 105, 143, 149
crossroads, 133
curiosity, 157, 175, 185
cynical, 119

D

daily review, 59, 177
day, 59, 109 127, 139, 145, 177
death grip, 103
decisions, 133
déjà vu, 69
delight, 33, 83
depleted, 9
detail, 11, 49, 145, 147, 161
direction, 27, 103, 133, 139, 167
disaster, 71
discernment, 73, 133
discomfort, 37
disorienting, 15, 137, 139, 141
disquiet, 77
distortion, 163
distraction, 145
disturbed, 43
doer, 109
donkey, 39
down, 141
dread, 63
dreamlike, 175
dress-up, 115
drop it, 55, 91

E

ease, 83, 119
emergency, 19
engagement, 91, 93, 185
enjoy the ride, 173, 179
enjoyment, 89, 173, 179
events, 157
expanding, 165
expanse, 165

F

fanfare, 91
fast brain, 17
favorite, 179
fear, 65
figure out, 61
filters, 163
fix, 85
fixed, 165
fleeting, 69
flow, 83, 127

focus, 103
force, 99
forever, 69
free will, 109
fresh eyes, 155
front and center, 55
full bray, 39
fully here, 47
future, 55
F-word, 31

G

gentle, 7
go before, 147
gratitude, 51, 57, 59, 77, 175, 177, 179, 183, 185, 187
gray, 33
grounding, 19, 65
guidance, 83, 133, 135, 139, 167

H

harm, 87
hearing, 53
heavy, 149
heckles, 43
help, 23
here, 45, 47, 53, 137
here and now, 53
hero complex, 91
honesty, 35, 105, 163
how, 121, 127
Hula-Hoop, 85
humiliation, 73
humility, 73, 159
humor, 75

I

illuminate, 155
in charge, 127
in love, 129
influence, 85
inner kid, 111, 113, 117
inspiration, 83, 117, 135, 155, 167
interaction, 83, 87, 89, 121, 147
interest, 167, 185
intuition, 135, 139

J

jaded, 119
jittery, 67
joy, 33, 173, 179, 181
judgy, 119

L

lamb, 113
laughter, 75
ledge, 25
legs, 65
let be, 81, 97
let go, 105, 107
life, 89, 129, 175
light, 139
listening, 13, 87
lists, 53, 77, 107, 177, 179, 181, 183, 185, 187
love, 59

M

mattering, 49, 61
meddling, 157
messy, 121
motion, 165
move through, 37, 41, 149
mystery, 127

N

new view, 71, 103, 133, 135, 137, 151
next, 3
nope, 29
not okay, 31, 41
not working, 99
now, 53, 55

O

objects, 11, 51
obsession, 23, 27
off-balance, 67
offering, 35, 77, 85, 95, 101, 107, 109, 127
okay, 15, 69
orbits, 159
others, 79, 81, 83, 87, 89, 121, 157
otter, 113
outcome, 105
overwhelm, 21

P

palpable, 141
passing, 69
past, 55, 181
pause, 87
perfection, 161
perspective, 71, 103, 133, 153, 155, 159, 163, 165
plant, 5
plugged in, 123
portable, 125
precision, 157
presence, 59, 141, 143, 147
present, 47, 143
prompts, 53, 77, 107, 149, 177, 179, 181, 183, 185, 187
protect, 43
pry open, 103
purpose, 167

Q

quiet, 3

R

reality, 163
reassurance, 69, 137, 141
reconnect, 33, 61
redirection, 103, 133, 135
refrain, 85

reframe, 153, 155, 159
relationship, 81, 121, 129
remembering, 179, 181
replay, 41
request, 181, 187
resistance, 39
rest, 7, 9, 13
right here, 53, 55
right-sized, 119
romance, 129

S

seeing, 11, 53, 71, 161
self-acceptance, 81, 113, 121, 149
self-care, 7, 13, 81, 113
self-centered, 157
self-honesty, 105, 163
self-love, 113, 129, 149
senses, 52
separate, 123
service, 91, 167
shaky, 67
shelter, 19
shit-storm, 35
shut it, 87
shying away, 175
silent-laugh, 75
singularity, 161
situation, 57, 139, 147, 149, 157
sloth, 7
small, 123
smelling, 53
smelly, 53
smooth, 67
solid, 165
sparkly, 49
spit, 37
spooked, 65
spot check, 53, 77, 177, 179, 185, 187
spring lamb, 113
squelchy, 97
stay, 45, 93, 149
stories, 71
subtle, 49
support, 87
surprise, 155
surrender, 101, 107, 109, 127, 149
surround, 43
swallow, 37

T

taking it personally, 159
tenderness, 113
thanks, 57, 65, 185
thinking, 43, 71
through, 37, 143
throw-down, 39
time, 55, 69
tired, 7
today, 109, 177, 183
toddler, 115
trash, 161
tree, 51
trust, 15, 101, 105, 125, 137, 147
truth, 105
twists and turns, 173

U

ugly, 121, 161
uncomfortable, 37, 119
underlayer, 49
unfamiliar, 137, 139, 141, 143
unfold, 147, 157
unhappy, 35
unrecognizable, 15, 143
unwilling, 99
up, 141
up close, 165

V

vibe, 67

W

wanting what I have, 129, 171
way through, 131, 133, 135, 139, 141
weather, 185
wigging out, 15
willingness, 99
wonder, 117
wood, 5
worry, 65, 77
worse, 41
wow, 149
wrecked, 67

Y

yes, 121, 169, 171, 173, 175
yield, 85